the world is brutal & you must be brave

introduction

here are 30 essays to keep in your bag, your car, your
bedside table — for when things get dark, like i know
they do.

on those days, i want you to be able to pull these words
up like a warm blanket, and hear my words telling you,
"you are not alone. no, you are not alone."

the world is brutal and you must be brave —
but, remember, we are here being brave with you.
look around. find the others. share your stories.
this is how we all go on.

as you read, you'll notice this book is separated into
three sections: sink, surface, swim. (or you can think
of them as accept/breathe/move.) that's just like life.
you must fully accept what is happening (sink), then
start rising (surface), and start propelling yourself (swim).
all are motion, and all are needed. try to do one without
the other two, and things may not work exactly right.

sink. surface. swim. you got this.

sending you big love,
lisbeth

contents

sink

the world is brutal & you must be brave
are you tired of your bullshit life?
you are not alone
fear, the monster
never apologize for crying
no damsels in distress
if
we tell ourselves
in the dark days
decide now

surface

finding your beautiful self again
the person who will free you
don't avoid the suck
stop trying to please everyone
hang onto your hope
on the corner of main and resilience
begin again
anger is a tool
don't save it for later
stop waiting for applause

swim

fight
it's you
if you can't hold on
second lives
one person
on faith
let us
shine
living well is the best revenge
the road ahead (being brave and going forward)

Also by Lisbeth Darsh:
Live Like That
Strong Starts in the Mind
Rise
The FUNctional Fitness Color & Activity Book for Adults
Strong Starts in the Mind: Workout Journal #1
Strong Starts in the Mind: Workout Journal #2

the world is brutal & you must be brave

Swim

Surface

Sink

the world is brutal & you must be brave

The world is brutal, and you must be brave.

I wish I could tell you otherwise. I wish I could fill your days with love and new barbells and beautiful, inspiring personal records. I wish I could tell you that the path to success is shiny and bright, and sunshine will come out of your sweet patootie. I wish I could tell you the dark days are over.

But that's not the truth. And stop listening to people who feed you that BS.

The world is often a much darker place. There are no unicorns: just horses with points glued on their noses.

The world can be a cold place. And vicious. And sometimes seemingly devoid of any real meaning. You can lose yourself in the world, searching for soul. But don't.

There is soul and you know how to look for it. You must look for it. You must find it.

Just because the world is brutal doesn't mean that you get to hide yourself off from it and live the life of the complainer, the person who never gets a break, the whiner with the perpetually doomed viewpoint, certain that life's sucker punch is always headed for them.

Don't search for pity.
Don't settle for consolation.
Fight for victory.

Salvation sits right at your feet.

It's just a stupid barbell, but it's one kick-ass weapon against the darkness.

Against the brutality of the world.
Against the brutality of your own thoughts.

Pick it up and the world gets better, at least in your own mind.

And that's where everything starts, isn't it? Change is born of one person, one mind, one action. Someone who says, "Yeah this sucks but I'm not going down."

The world is brutal, and you must be brave.

But you have a barbell. You can do something. And then another thing. And another.

you change.
things change.
we change.
get on it.

are you tired of your bullshit life?

Are you living a life of quiet desperation?

Stop that shit.

All over the place, people talk about their unhappiness, and they mention the ways they are often unknowingly sacrificing their happiness because they feel they have to. You hear words like:

Expectations

Obligations

The kids come first

The spouse/boyfriend/girlfriend comes first

And a thousand other reasons ("I can't move" "I can't get a different job" "I have to do this" and others).

It's not that these are not important things (they are), it's that something else always comes first. Always. And, at times, it feels somewhat like martyrs celebrating their own funeral pyres.

Now, I'm not telling them — or you — to be a selfish jackwagon. I'm not telling you to stop serving people. I'm not telling you that you must place your happiness before everyone else's.

I'm not even sure happiness works that way. In fact, I'm pretty sure that happiness is what shows up when you're so busy getting stuff done that you forgot to look for happiness. Boom! You turn around and happiness is sitting on the front porch swing, smiling and popping the top on a cool, refreshing beverage.

But what I am telling you is that if you're living a life of quiet desperation, you can stop and change.

You don't have to be unhappy.
You don't have to live a life you don't want to live.

Like I've said before, happiness is not given, happiness is chosen. If you're making the choice each day to live a life that you think you should be living instead of the real life you are meant to live, then maybe it's time to make some changes, darling.

See, bullshit lives don't simply fly away like errant pigeons in a parking lot. They don't magically disappear or transform themselves through no effort of your own. Nope.

Bullshit lives are changed through hard, dirty work.

Sweat, tears, tons of work, numerous sleepless nights, and too many sorrow-filled dawns — that's how bullshit lives are changed. But you have to make a decision first.

You have to decide that what you have is:
not enough for your heart
not enough for your life
not enough for your soul.

That you'd rather go down swinging than put up with one more day of a life that smothers you with its emptiness and stuffs sand down your own throat.

It's your unhappiness or you. Only one gets to win. And sitting silently seething is no way to spend your beautiful life.

Nor is your life meant to be spent in the continual act of complaint.

your life is meant to be spent in joy!

As a friend facing a major life decision said to me one day, "I don't want to be one of those people who sits and complains. I want to live."

So, you might have some decisions in front of you, but that doesn't mean you have to get in the car and drive away from your life. But it does mean maybe you should check the map and rev your engine a little — because even small adjustments can make a big difference in your outlook.

Like Thoreau wrote all those years ago, "Those same stars twinkle over other fields than these." Imagine yourself in those fields and under those stars. Feels good, right? Maybe you can find a way there. Tell me if you do — because I know how you feel and I'm always rooting for you.

you are not alone

You are not alone.

I feel like I could say these words 100 times a day, and still it would be not enough.

You are not alone.

I say it to myself.
I say it other people.
I say it to my dog.
(I also tell him I like "his people" and to pass that word among them, but he just stares at me with one ear up/one ear down and I don't think he does anything with that nugget of information.)

You are not alone.

Why do I feel compelled to say this? Why do I try to build community everywhere I go, since my days as a child in nursery school right to this moment now in my hands? Why can't I stop?

Because you are not alone. And I am not alone.

Because I know how you feel in the dark moments, when the curtain has descended and all is blackness around, and you wonder if anyone knows, if anyone has ever felt this way, if anyone cares, if life will ever be sweet again, taste sweet, sound sweet, feel sweet, in this or any other lifetime.

I know how black the night gets. I know how silent the room gets. I know how sharp the pain is when your heart breaks — and it breaks a hundred times a day.

I know how sad and alone you feel. Because I feel that way, too.

And the only way that I rise above, that I keep breathing, keep living, keep existing until I find my way to laughter to lust to love to compassion or confrontation or coexistence again is simply this this this this: I remember that I am not alone.

so, believe me, you are not alone.

Keep going, Skippy. And so will I.

fear, the monster

You're unsure. You're scared.

We all are.

welcome to the society of everyone.

I'm so scared in life sometimes that I hold my breath, like a monster is just outside my door and he'll hear me so closely is he listening. (I know, I flatter myself that the monster cares so much about me that he listens and waits, and waits and listens, like I am the most important creature he must chase today.)

But I always open the door and run into the world, the void, the opportunity, the moment. I cannot help myself.

I am foolish that way
Or romantic
Call it what you will.

(Maybe you are the same way. We are stupid and smart in the same moment, like genius children who can drive and buy things in the grocery store but who can still not figure out how to avoid broken hearts and sadness in the daily grind.)

The truth is that sometimes this monster of my dreams is there, and he gets me. He may not drag me under the bed like I imagine he would, with his green toes and his hairy hands firm upon my warm flesh, but I end up there in my mind anyhow, fighting, fighting, fighting with my fear to get back above the surface of this floor, up back to the safety of the soft sheets and the ever cool other side of the pillow — the place where the monster does not live and I can only hear his breathing but I am safe, or as safe as I can hope to be.

Safe for now.

I live. I breathe and go on.

At least so far.

I'm guessing that if you're reading this, so do you.

Fear is the monster, but we know how to beat him.

never apologize for crying

Never apologize for tears.

No, really. Don't apologize for crying.

Don't sniffle and say "I'm sorry for crying" to your friends or your partner or your mom or your brother or even the clerk at the Safeway who is looking at you with a tilted head and asking, "Honey, are you okay?" as she slowly places the dish detergent into your reusable shopping bag. It's just a moment. You are not the first person to cry in a supermarket, and you won't be the last. At any given moment, there are probably five people in that store who are fighting back tears and another two on the verge of losing it altogether as they move among the bok choy and the broccoli. Life is not easy for any of us.

Tears are not something to regret. A showing of sadness does not need to be forgiven. Sadness is allowed, even necessary in a way that not many of us fully understand.

Perhaps this world would be better if we cried more, not less. Perhaps we would do more for each other if we felt more. (Don't listen to those misguided fools who speak of the weakening of the world and urge you to "harden up." This world, like you, needs to be tough at the right moments and soft at the right moments, but we can each figure that out for ourselves.)

So, abandon your penchant for apology when physical manifestation of your emotional vulnerability presents itself at inopportune moments. You are fine.

Tears are a sign of how deeply you feel life: this is a good thing.
You are not numb.
You are not detached.
You are not uncaring.

You are here, breathing fully and deeply and gloriously with a beating heart that aches and hurts and lives. Tears are simply proof that you still care.

how wonderful that you can feel life so much.

Let the tears come, and let them go. Hold your head up. You got this.

no damsels in distress

This isn't a fairytale.

I can't manufacture hope out of nothing, like a blanket out of invisible threads woven on some magic loom. There are no magic beans, and there's no long-haired prince to ride up and save you.

Even if your life is seriously fucked, you will have to save yourself.
That sucks, right?

Or maybe it's the best thing ever.

See, when you're given something you never value it as much as when you earn it. You know that. So, earn it. Earn your happy ending, just like you had to earn that personal record on your deadlift or your last promotion. Put your heart and soul and all the effort you can muster into what needs fixing in your life.

If it's your business: head down, shoulder to the wheel, start pushing.
If it's your relationships: head up, ears open, find out what's wrong, and figure out how you can adjust your own behavior and make things better. (Read that sentence again — it works for your business too.)

Don't be the damsel in distress, because you know what? Everybody secretly hates that gal. Whining and crying and wanting somebody else to do the work: what kind of attitude is that?

Adjust your own attitude. Weave your own hope.

life will get better when you get better.

if

If you're lost, join the club. We all are.

It's just that some of us are pretending not to be. Or we do a great job of looking confident, self-assured, and kick-ass. But inside? We're a mess like everybody else.

If you're down-hearted, pick yourself up. Stop complaining. That's the first step to feeling better. Keep telling your victim story and you stay the victim. Move forward. New memories are made every day.

even if your life has been horrible, it doesn't have to stay that way.

Change your thoughts, change your words, change your mojo, now.

If you're on top of the world and everything is going absolutely fantastic for you, be grateful. Boast less, give thanks more. Most people won't tell you when you're being a jackass, so you better learn to cap that tendency yourself. (And if you do have someone in your life who will tell you when you're being a fool? Be grateful for them. The truth hurts, but it will save you.) Yes, it's great to be happy. But make sure to share the wealth, and keep an eye on the redline on your Jackass Meter.

If you're reading these words, be grateful you have the time and ability to do so. You're probably not worried about your safety, your next meal, or if you'll see another day. There's no IED buried on your road, no IV bag hooked up to your arm, and you probably have enough money to go to the grocery store and buy a healthy meal.

Perspective: eat it every morning. Then go forth and make something of yourself and the day.

we tell ourselves

We tell ourselves all sorts of things.
"This weight is too heavy for me."
"I'm not a fast runner."
"I'm not that smart."
Well, screw that.

every time you tell yourself bullshit, you're limiting yourself.

Just because something was, doesn't mean it has to be. I'm slow as heck when I run. What's that mean I should do to improve? Run more. Get better. Get more efficient. Get faster.

You're weak at writing, or math, or braiding your daughter's hair. What should you do? Tell yourself that you suck? Obsess about your failures? No.

Practice more. Get better. Get more efficient. Get stronger. Stop telling yourself what you are not, and start telling yourself what you could be.

Then (and this part is key): work like hell to become that.

in the dark days

in the dark days of our lives, even the smallest piece of light is critical.

You won't get far without light. You'll stay in your bed, your house, your hole, your rut, the place that feels warm and safe and yet is killing you hour by hour, day by day, year by year.

You know the hole is wrong. On some level, you know it, just like you know you're not supposed to eat out of that ice cream carton with just a spoon. ("Get a dish like a civilized person," your mother would say, but she'd also tell you to sit up straight — and that is just not happening right now.)

Still you stay in your hole.

But one day the dark is just too much.

You catch a glimpse of the light and you want it. You tire of the dark and the feeling that life is never going to get any better. You decide to make it different. To will yourself out of the hole. To change the sky from grey to blue with your hands if you have to. You're done with dark.

But, until that day comes, find a flashlight or a match or a spark. A book, a poem, a song. A crumpled up old love note from a long-past lover whom you don't want anymore but whose words can still help, still remind you that you are a thing of desire, that you can make pulses race, that you can thrill people just by smiling at them. Remember that.

Keep a piece of the light in your pocket until you see the sun again.

decide now

If you don't like your life, change it.
If you don't like some part of your life, work on it and change it.
Life is way too short to be miserable.

Don't give excuses about how you can't change. Excuses are just a way of convincing yourself to feel okay about not doing anything.

Well, it's not okay to live a crappy life.
It's not okay to live an unfulfilled life.
It's not okay to be unhappy and refuse to do anything about it.

Do my words anger you or make you squirm? If so, maybe you have excuses.
Maybe you've reasoned with yourself as to why you can't make changes.
Maybe you're settling for being less than you can be.

I know because I used to be you. I had a "nice life" that was eating at my soul every hour of the day, every day of the year. Until one day I said no more, and I broke free. It was painful, and it took a while, but life got better and I was finally living the life I was meant to live.

So now I'm here and I know what you can do: Decide to change.
Or don't.

And, if the answer is "I can't change," then enjoy your mediocre life. Spend your time typing inanities on your phone, being jealous of other people, and dreaming about what could have been.

Or, there's a better life. A better way. A better you. But you have to stand up and grab your chance.

Clean up your attitude.
Clean up your words.
Clean up your diet.
Clean up your relationships.
Clean up your life.

It can all get better or it can all get worse.

you decide. right now.

Swim

Surface

Sink

finding your beautiful self again

If you lost her, today might be the day you find her. You know who I'm talking about — the gal inside you, the one you used to know, the brave and fearless one who was going to conquer the world and do everything her way.

What happened to her?

Work. Family. Stress. Life.

She got busy, and then she got tired.

Then suddenly it felt like time ran out. Gone. No matter how many times you flipped the hourglass, there weren't enough minutes in the day to call that crazy girl back.

She showed up in flashes sometimes — at the gym, or alone in your car, or after a few drinks at a party. She appeared and people's eyes lit up. They wanted more of this gorgeous creature — this sparkling part of you, your true and beautiful self … but that was so hard, so risky, so dangerous. Easier to be like the others. Easier to fit in, to not get too risky, to stay safe. Life was hard enough.

And so mostly, that girl was AWOL. You were AWOL from your one and only life.

Like many people, you settled. It happens. Don't beat yourself up about it. Those years gave you good things, too.

But here's the thing: you don't have to stay settled.

Look at the Earth. Everything looks and seems so permanent … and then there's an earthquake. A shifting of the plates, a rising of the Earth in places where the crust can no longer contain the stresses and the shifting, and so there is a break. And the Earth breathes again. Yes, there is damage (hopefully not too much) but it is inevitable. This is Nature taking her path. And so too must you.

it's not too late to find your beautiful self again.

She's waiting. And you can either let her continue to chase you in the night, or you can turn and talk to her right now.

the person who will free you

The person who will free you is you.

Stop thinking it's someone else, or that it could be anyone else. We get this not-so-hot idea in life from somewhere (Our family? Our friends? Our culture?) that we are not the hero. That we should wait for the hero.

Guess what? You are the flippin' hero in your life. You. Not someone else. You.

We don't have to accept this idea that God or the universe will save us, that some divine event or series of events will put us on the right path and lead us to the Promised Land.

Because maybe that's not exactly it either.

Maybe there is no "secret." Or maybe "the secret" looks a bit more like hard work, laughter, love, kindness, and cold beer on the front porch afterward.

Maybe to get to the Promised Land, you have to throw yourself on the line like Bruce Springsteen sang about:
"There's a dark cloud rising from the desert floor
I packed my bags and I'm heading straight into the storm
Gonna be a twister to blow everything down
That ain't got the faith to stand its ground."

Head straight into the storm.

Or, start your own storm, and call down the thunder too — the thunder from within yourself.

because the person who will free you ... is you.

don't avoid the suck

You can't avoid the suck.

You want to think you can. You want to think there are ways and methods and things and products that can help you avoid the suck and just get all the good stuff in life — like picking the good caramels in a box of chocolates and leaving those candies with the weird pink fluffy stuff inside. But life doesn't work that way. And most great things don't come about that way.

Some gyms and magazines will tell you that you can avoid the suck — do it in fewer days, fewer hours, less pain.

"Success in 3 easy steps!" "Success in 30 days!"

They think you're stupid and weak. But you're not. You know that. You also know life is hard.

You know that you have to work repeatedly (and really hard) for whatever you want. And you know you won't always get it. That's part of the suck. But you also know that it's all worth trying for, and that if you really try — put your heart and your body and your soul on the line — that you'll get ... something. It might not always be what you were aiming for: it might be less, but in that less it might be more.

Huh?

Think of it this way: Ever lose at something? Think you're going to come in first and you come in fifth? Or last? Ever learn a ton from that performance? Yup. You came up with less, but you got more.

What you set your sights on is not always what you get.

Sometimes you go through the suck and the prize at the end is totally and wholly different than whatever you had your eye on. That's okay.

suckage always teaches a lesson. you just have to train yourself to look for it.

Stop trying to avoid the suck.
The good stuff is on the other side of it.

stop trying to please everyone

No matter what you say or do, someone won't like it. You either said it too strong, too weak, or not just right enough. You were too pushy, not forceful enough, not funny enough, not fit enough, notnotnotnotnot.

Oh, who cares?

The point is YOU said it. YOU did it.

You. Not them. They just sat back and criticized. That's super-easy to do. Everyone doesn't have to like you. Everyone shouldn't like you. That's not how life works, and that's okay. There are people who hate vanilla ice cream and deadlifts. Go figure.

So, the next time someone disagrees with you or makes a snide remark or throws a rock at you, don't stress. Smile and ask them what they've created or done lately. But don't wait for the reply, because there likely won't be one.

just get back to doing.

This life is made up of people who take risks, get real, get vulnerable, throw their hearts on the table, kick ass, persevere and just plain rock ... and it's made up of people who complain and do nothing.

The only thing you really have to figure out is which group you're in, and whether you want to stay there.

hang onto your hope

"Hang onto your hopes, my friend. That's an easy thing to say but if your hopes should pass away, simply pretend that you can build them again."
— Paul Simon

If only life could be so easy, right?

But it's not. No, the extinguishing of hope is one of the crueler sounds in life. Because hope usually doesn't scream. She limps and fades. No crash or bang to end it all. No leap off the cliff with a dive towards the water, an arc, a sign of beauty before destruction and annihilation.

No, hope dies slowly and quietly, the most painful of death, with nary a hospice aide in sight. No morphine. You are the hospice aide of your hope, and you nurse, nurse, nurse her until she can breathe no more and she dies.

And then you hope you'll find a new hope. Something sitting there alone and shiny, suddenly there in front of you like a dropped $100 bill or a lottery ticket that gets stuck under your windshield wiper by some strong wind.

Maybe that's your new hope. Maybe you'll take her out on the town. "Here's my new hope!" People like shows. We are all drawn to each other's hope, those of us who still have hearts left.

Yet it's far more likely that your new hope won't wander into your life like that.

most hopes need a little work to get found, so you best get moving.

Hope comes when you're working so hard you forgot to look for her. But if you find her? Hang onto your hope, my friend.

on the corner of main and resilience

Sometimes, life is hard. So fucking hard.

The world comes at you big and bold and loud, with troubles and problems and heartbreaking sadness, and you sit amidst the noise and color and motion and you just want it all to slow down for a moment, to settle, to be so not in-your-face. Only for a little bit.

Can't everybody stop the carnival madness for one second?

But you don't get that. Because the world doesn't listen, no matter how loud you yell.

You teeter on the edge of losing it, on breaking down and crying alone in your car as the traffic sits at the light and your turn signal goes blink-blink-blink and you're not even sure how long that's been on and it might have been since that last exit and why can't you ever remember to turn it off? You wonder how you're going to make it through the next hour, let alone the rest of life.

And how did you even get here?

On those days, when it all feels like hell, do this: look for the small victory, the tiny win, the one thing you did right.

One thing.

It can be as simple as tying your shoes, because some days that seems to be the only thing you did right — tie your shoes. Everything else is screwed up, but damn, Skippy, you got yourself some tied shoes.

Hold onto the simple things, to whatever you did right. Cling to that. It might seem stupid and silly but when things aren't going your way, if you want to turn it all around, you will have to focus on what is going your way and build from there.

You got up this morning.
You dressed yourself.
And who knows, maybe tomorrow you'll put your shirt on right the first time too.

buck up. you still don't suck as much as you think you do.

begin again

So, your life sucks.
Begin again.
So, your heart is down.
Begin again.

Your job, your romance, your relationships, your bank account, and everything that you think is your life may have just fallen to total and irrevocable garbage ... but you know what? It's not really your life. Your life is your heart beating and your lungs filling with air and your brain overflowing with a million thoughts and emotions.

If you're reading this, you're still breathing. So, pick yourself up off the floor. Wipe the dirt off your butt and ... begin again.

Each and every day. Every single time you fail. Begin again. As long as you draw breath in this world. Nobody said it was going to be easy for you. Nobody said it was going to be rainbows and roses and (creepy) clowns. Sure, nobody said it would be this hard, either. But you woke up today. So many people were not so lucky.

begin again, always.

Grab hold of that new chance with both hands and don't you let it go.

anger is a tool

The world tells you not to be angry. You're not supposed to have anger, but you do. It's a basic human emotion, yet you're not supposed to show it. So, like many people, you turn that anger inside yourself. You turn it into shame. Or guilt. Or sadness.

And that's just all sorts of wrong. Anger isn't a moral sentence. It's not a weakness to have it or show it. Anger is just an emotion. It comes and it should go. But denying it is not the answer.

Why do we think we can suppress a basic human emotion?
Deny it.
Stuff it down.
Eliminate it.
That's so stupid.

When someone asks me, "Why are you angry?" I ask them, "Why are you not?"

Anger is okay to have. It's okay to co-exist with. Use anger for its purpose — to identify something that bothers you, and then to drive forward. Use it for that, and then move on.

And if you have extra anger that you can't get rid of? The barbell will take it.

Put that anger in deadlifts or back squats or push jerks. The trail will take it, too. And the pavement. Put that anger into your sprints, or try to wear it out over the miles. Ride a bike. There's no therapy like mountain-bike therapy — plus you get to shout and growl if you want and nobody looks at you weird if you do.

Just don't try to deny the existence of anger. Look at it, acknowledge it, use it, and let it go.

anger is a tool. pick it up and put it back down.

Good luck, my friends.

don't save it for later

Do you save it for later?

Is this your mindset? At least some of the time? In your workout, in your home, in your heart?

"I can't go all out here. Got to save something for later."
"I can't tell her how I feel. Maybe later."
"I should save these old fat pants. I might wear them again one day."

Do you hold yourself back (just a little)? Do you play it safe all the time? Stop it. Most of the time, you're doing yourself no favors. In fact, you'd probably do better by going a little harder, giving a little more, being more of you.

Not all of the time, but most. The stuff you're "saving for later" might be weighing you down. Perhaps it's time to open your wingspan just a touch more.

This life is short. No matter how long it seems in any given moment, this life is over in a flash for all of us. So, save when it makes sense, like with money and time.

But everything else?

be smart, be courageous, be bold.
throw everything you've got on the line and watch life reply.

Sometimes you're going to make it, sometimes you're going to win, sometimes you're going to be smiling and shaking your head at how lucky you are.

And sometimes you'll be sitting there feeling like a truck ran you over, wondering what the hell you did wrong.

It's all good.

Just don't save it all for later. Later may never come.

But now? Now is waiting for you to kick ass.

stop waiting for applause

Stop waiting for applause — in the gym and in every facet of your life. Stop waiting for the camera shot and the "good job."

In fact, if someone says "good job" to you, ignore them. (Or just give the requisite thank-you.) You don't need "good job" — you need to get better. You need to do better. And in order to do something well, you need to know what you did wrong.

So, when you're done with a lift, or a race, or a presentation, or a paper, or even putting your kids to bed, don't sit there and wait for someone to tell you that you did a good job. That's only going to help your ego, not your future performance.

Look for the ones who can help. We all need helpers.

The best ones aren't the coaches waiting with a "You did great!" when your lift looked like garbage. Or the ones who beat you down, no matter what, and never have a good word to say.

The best coaches (and the best friends and partners and loved ones) look at us with a tilted head and a smile. They fix us with a steely gaze and give us the truth, as they see it:
what we did right,
what we did wrong,
what we need to work on for next time.

they love us enough to tell us how we can improve.

Sometimes, those aren't easy words to hear. But you need to really hear them. The best coaches in this life know when to kick you in the ass and when to hug you. Let them. You're going to be a far better person if you do.

Swim

Surface

Sink

fight

Fight.

I'm talking to you. Fight.

Don't let this world get the best of you.
Don't let it take you alive.
Don't let this world beat you until you give up.

No matter what happens, you keep going.

Sure, life is going to pummel you, but dammit fight back. Kick, scratch, claw, do whatever it takes to keep breathing, keep going, keep living.

All you have — all you've ever had, really — is heart. A whole lot of heart.

Don't give it up now.

many people have given up on this life, on their loves, on this world. don't be one of them.

Don't walk this earth with a life foregone but not yet ended.
Don't settle for less.
Don't settle for bullshit.
Don't settle at all.

Fight.

Refuse to be defeated.

Refuse to go down.

Refuse to be one of the ones who never really made it, who never really got what they wanted, who lived a life less than they could have.

Fight until your last moment, your last thought, your last breath.

Rage on.

Don't just live. Rage.

The light only dies if you let it.

Don't let it. Fight.

it's you

It's all bullshit.

All of this stuff that people try to sell you. All this talk that this or that or the other thing is going to do "it": help your business explode, make your workout easier, bring you love or success on a silver platter. The million pitches you get about some fantastic product that will make your life become the stuff that people dream of.

Many people want to sell you the answer, and many people want to buy it.

But there is no answer that can be sold or bought. Because the answer is easy and yet so hard.

You have to be better.
Better. You. Every single day.

Maybe better than the next person, better than that guy over there, better than the woman sitting next to you. But — most importantly — better than yourself. And that's not the answer that some people want to hear — because it's hard, really hard.

See, it's not your business system or some magic words or potions that will create untold health and wealth and success for you and everyone you touch. You can't buy it in a download. It doesn't matter which management system you use, or whether you read that book that everyone talked about, or if you used your thoughts to manifest reality. No, it's something much simpler. And way more scary.

It's YOU.

whether your life is a flaming success or a burnt-out failure, it's all up to you.

It's not the excuses you give to others, or the explanations you try to sell yourself late at night when the events of the day keep spinning in your head. It's not what you tell yourself when your failure keeps chasing you right up until dreamland.

Whether you live a life of noisy mediocrity, interrupted by bouts of public drunkenness — or whether you grab your goals, one after another, with steely precision — it's up to you.

Stop looking to buy success. And, for heaven's sake, stay away from the people trying to sell it to you.

Start working on your skills instead.

You want to be better? Fantastic. Get to work on you.

if you can't hold on?

If you can't hold on?

Hold on.

If you think you can't make it one more second, one more breath, one more moment?

Yes, you can.

If you're sure that this next day, this next heartache, this next workout will kill you?

It won't.

Life is full of exaggerations. We are full of exaggerations. Everything is so bad, so tough, so horrible — but, often, it's only our minds making it so. I bet we all (each one of us) are far stronger than we ever realize — physically, mentally, spiritually.

The tank really isn't empty. You're just being weak.

Figure out what you need to do to get strong again: maybe it's air or water or rest or food you need. Maybe it's twenty hugs, or one good soul-filling squeeze with two hands and no pat on the back.

But it's something.

Figure it out and get back to work.

life does not improve unless you improve.

second lives

We all have a chance at a second life.

No, I'm not talking religious dogma or zombie stuff or some kind of medical resurrection, but a life you live after you try something else. Your second life isn't necessarily better or worse than your first life (you might like both just fine) but, usually, it's more you.

Many of us grow up with some preconceived notion of who we should be. It might be some idea foisted upon us by parents or siblings or our community — or, often, just ourselves. We think we must be this thing. So we aim, and try, and become that thing. Only to find ourselves unhappy, or just discontented, or downright miserable.

And we break.

And we realize things have to change, if we are to live, or at least not go mad.

And going mad all at once, or little by little, piece by piece, your soul drifting away from you and floating downstream, seems very real — you could paint it in a watercolor, so vivid is the image — that you awake at night, the bedclothes sweaty with your fear, the fright clutched in your hands.

But you forge on.

Your life is not without color, but the colors seem flat, and you don't even totally realize the utter blandness of your landscape.

Then something happens and you catch a glimpse of what life could be. It's almost scary to glimpse. But it's there. And now you have to see more of it, so you keep heading that way, working, charging, fighting until it becomes more than a dream. A plan. Now you have a plan and you work harder.

One day, you get there.

It might be quick, or it might be really long and painful, but you get there. You have a second life. And, often, it's better than the first. Why? Because maybe your old life sucked, but you couldn't really admit it. That was too hard. It was something you worked on for SO long. How could you have been wrong? Admitting you lost your way is difficult, but you do it. And you breathe in the sweet air of your second life. Air never tasted so delicious.

A friend of mine once said this to me, as I stood in the swamp of self-doubt, sure that my first life was not who I was, but not yet certain of how to get out of the bog and start on the dry path to my second life: "You have to let go of your preconceived notions of who you are, who you should be, and go with what works for you now."

I listened, and did — and somehow I made it.

So did many others: their stories litter the world in some sort of trail that you could follow if you could see the markers, the signs, the clues that point you towards the path you really want to take, not just the obvious, paved road you've been walking down.

I guess what I'm trying to say with probably far too many words, is that if you're somewhere in your life where the vague ghosts of discontent flutter in your stomach daily and haunt your dreams at night, take heart.

you are alive. there is hope. work, and find your way.

one person

Sometimes all it takes is one person. Sometimes you can do it all alone. But sometimes you just need one other person to believe, one other person to give a damn, one other person to say "Keep going" or "I know how you feel" or simply "Hell yeah."

One person to tell you "I've been broken, too."

One person.

How simple is that and yet how incredibly difficult? Most of us are independent by nature. We want to believe we can do it all alone, without the help of anyone else. We want to do it all by ourselves. For us, the weakness is not in our efforts, but in our wanting, in our need for anyone or anything else in this life.

yet one person can make all the difference in our workout, in our day, in our week, in our life.

One person to cheer. One person to coach. One person to basically give a damn about us. Whether you're in the gym or at work or at home or online, listen for that one person. And be that one person for someone else.

on faith

I'm driving along and Bruce Springsteen is singing about having faith.
Not faith like Bible faith or Jesus faith or Allah faith or Buddha faith.
Just faith. *"I still got a little faith but what I need is some proof tonight."*
That's kind of how I think of faith, also — not in a religious or spiritual
manner, but as a belief in people.

A belief in the strength and essential goodness of myself, and of you, and you
and you and you.
A belief in this world.
A belief in lightness emerging from darkness.
A belief in lightness triumphing over darkness.

I understand the comfort that belief can bring.

Communication coaches will tell you not to use the words "I think" or "I believe"
because you don't need them, that your argument is stronger when you simply
state everything as fact. Maybe that's why I don't like communication coaches
all that much. They don't understand my heart. They don't get my soul. They
make me efficient by making me like everyone else.

Beliefs are powerful. They drive us. And "I believe" is a powerful statement
to yourself, even more than to anyone else.

i want you to say "i believe." i want you to think about what you believe and say it.

So, make your list. Start with five things. Tell me what you believe. Make another list. Tell yourself more things. And, more importantly, tell yourself each and every day.

Here's mine for right now:
1. I believe in the basic goodness of every human.
2. I believe civil discussion is possible, but we must insist upon it without getting angry about it.
3. I believe politeness can be the gateway drug to cooperation.
4. I believe that people can change if they really want to change.
5. I believe that forgiveness is ridiculously hard but phenomenally important.

What are your beliefs?

let us

let us resolve not to beat ourselves up.

Let us decide that each effort, fully given, is enough.

Let us not engage in self-imposed mental cruelty whereby we say to ourselves, "If only I had done it this way" or "Why the heck didn't I do that?" over and over in some kind of self-punishment circle of hell.

Let us not call ourselves names or speak poorly about our abilities.
No "I'm so weak."
No "I'm pathetic."
No "I'll never be able to do this."

None of that helps, really. We are who we are. We have what we have.
All we can do is give each effort fully, totally, in that moment. And that will be enough. It must be enough.

Some days, we will be wonderful. Some days, we will suck. That's life.
Just work hard and try to get over it. Whether it's in the gym or in our lives as partners and parents and workers and sons and daughters, we must give all we have and then walk away from the effort.

Learn what we can.
Improve what we must.
But not become our own worst enemy.

We must take what we should from an experience and no more.

Mark Twain once said, "We should be careful to get out of an experience only the wisdom that is in it — and stop there; lest we be like the cat that sits down on a hot stove lid. She will never sit on a hot stove lid again — and that is well; but also she will never sit down on a cold one anymore."

Let us remember what we can and forget what we must.

Let us be human to ourselves.

Let us achieve, but never forget the sweetness and utter importance of kindness. Without it, life just isn't the same. Let us always remember that.

shine

Shine.
No matter what anybody tries to do to you today. No matter how anyone or anything tries to destroy you. No matter how much life seems to gang up on you and conspire to bring you down. Don't let life do that. Don't let anyone or anything drag you down today.
Shine.

Take the blows and stand back up. Stagger if you have to, but get your feet under you again and surge forward. Sure, you might be punch drunk.
You might stumble. You might think, "How much more can they do to me?"
The answer is not what you want to hear, so stop asking. Just fight back in your own way.
Shine.

Don't look to crush the other guy. Look to crush your own weaknesses, your own insecurities, your own doubts and fears and failures. Because the other guy — your opponent — is going to change constantly. By the hour. By the day. By the year. But you will always be there. So you need to get as strong as you can get.

If this world was made up of paper tigers, you would be the biggest, baddest motherfucker ever. But this world has real tigers and folks who don't want the best for you. Rise above them. Crawl above them. Break free of their darkness and head to the light.

make your own light. invite others to come with you.

Shine.

living well is the best revenge

We all have someone who did us wrong.

Someone who walked into our lives and did horrible things, and then walked casually out again, so easy for them, like a summer breeze lightly lifting the bedroom curtains. Someone whose deeds still weigh on us long after they are gone.

Many of us learn to forgive and forget, but some folks have a harder time with that.

If you can't forget what happened to you, then remember that feeling. Really remember it and use it.

if you can't rise above, then rise through.

The next time you're stuck in the middle of a bad workout or a bad day? Think of who hurt you. The next time you don't want to pick up the barbell and do nine more thrusters? Remember that jerk. The next time the workout is about to defeat you? When you're tired and ready to yell "No mas" and just give up? Remember and rise up for one more rep. And another. And another.

Because if you're going to keep the anger — if you won't give it up — then make damn sure you use it.

If you can't get rid of the pain, then use the pain.

Use every last breath and hurt and gut punch that ever came your way. Remember when you were down and they were kicking the snot out of you.

Remember it all. And let it drive you through and beyond. If you're going to carry that weight, use it.

Then, if you do the hard work to get past it, one day like a freakin' miracle, you'll find you can't find the pain anymore. It will be gone — disappeared — like it rode that breeze out a different open window.

And it will be absolutely no coincidence that you'll find you don't need the pain anymore either. You can do better without it. You'll be free and so much stronger than you ever were before.

They say living well is the best revenge. Maybe lifting well is the way to get there.

the road ahead (being brave and going forward)

You read. You listen. You watch.

You soak in the wisdom and the knowledge, but then you are on your own and you have one pressing question that beats between your ears, that drowns out music everywhere until you answer it: What do you do now?

What's the first step?
What does brave look like going forward?
How will you know you're on the right path?

The answers are all yours.

You will know the first step when it appears. Watch, and let it. Swallow hard and step forward.

You will know what brave looks like when you're so scared — SO SCARED — and you move forward anyhow.

You might screw it all up. That's okay. Keep going. This is what brave looks like: not perfect and never finished.

The right path looks like this: you'll never know for sure, but you'll feel the right steps.

They don't feel like pain.
They feel like deep sleep.
They taste like air and sunlight and crisp apples on a New York fall day.

Or at least that's what the right path tastes like for me — but it might taste different to you, and that's okay. But you'll have to keep your ears open, because it will be the absence of noise that lets you know you're doing it right for you.

That's weird, right?

It is.

But when you hit the right path for you, the universe stops yelling.

listen for the quiet. feel the calm deep in your soul. it will be your answer.

THE
WORLD
IS
BRUTAL
AND
YOU
MUST
BE
BRAVE

*to love to love to love until the point of breaking
... and then to love more.*

Lisbeth Darsh is the author of seven books and the popular fitness/inspiration blog **Words With Lisbeth**. A former executive at CrossFit Inc, she has also been a fitness coach/ gym owner, an English professor, and a military officer, with degrees from Vassar College (BA) and California State University at Dominguez Hills (MA). She lives in the Santa Cruz mountains of California with her two children.

Other books by Lisbeth Darsh:
Live Like That
Strong Starts in the Mind
Rise
The FUNctional Fitness Color & Activity Book for Adults
Strong Starts in the Mind: Workout Journal #1
Strong Starts in the Mind: Workout Journal #2